THE 7 POINTS OF Write

An Essential Guide to:
Mastering the Art of Storytelling,
Developing Strong Characters,
and Setting Memorable Scenes

DANIEL MIDDLETON

7-11
Press

For information about this and other 711 Press titles and products, visit us on the World Wide Web at:
www.711press.com

Cover and Interior Design by *Scribe Freelance*
www.scribefreelance.com

ISBN: 978-1-935702-10-8

Published in the United States of America

For my wife, Karen,
without whom I would not have made it this far;
and my daughter, Naomi,
who gives me reason to go even farther.

Contents

INTRODUCTION

WHILE THERE ARE droves of "how-to" books currently on the market that focus on writing well and liberally dispense varied instructions—among them the use of proper word choices, avoiding wordiness, employing active verbs and active voice, and other writerly rules and elements of writing style—this book will focus on something those books do not offer: how to tap into the writer in all of us and unearth the interesting stories and characters that are buried deep within. How you can approach this from a technical standpoint—an area that concerns the mechanics of written language, which necessitates a knowledge of proper grammar, usage, sentence structure, and the principles of composition, phrasing, punctuation, etc.—involves lessons that can be learned elsewhere. What this book will attempt to do is teach you how to draw from the deep well of experience that is at the core of every human being and couple it with imagination to effectively tell a memorable tale, regardless of the genre you choose to write in.

If you are a member of the human race who draws breath on a daily basis and can confirm that you have lived a life on any level and have associated with any number of fellow human beings in whatever manner during the course of that life, then you are capable of telling a story, and a compelling one at that, based on, fueled by, or inspired by those experiences.

Throughout my career as a professional book editor, I have come to understand and recognize the nuances of quality fiction and have pinpointed the necessary ingredients a writer needs in order to attain a lofty level of storytelling. You see, one of the main problems many fiction writers face today is a lack of skill when it comes to conveying their thoughts with power and conviction. Many times I have read scenes that fall flat for a variety of reasons, be it weak character sketching, the inability to effectively describe scenery or action, and, not least, poor delivery of dialogue, among many other classic examples. In order to allow your readers to come away satisfied after reading your book, or compel them to reread passages for the sheer power and beauty contained within them, you have to tap into your hidden depths of experience. You must draw power from within, by envisioning a scene so clearly that you begin to act very much like a reporter who is trying to jot down as much of what he or she is witnessing as possible, and as accurately as he or she can.

Bonus Point

Great writers aren't born; They're made

That is exactly what I will teach you to do!

The seven *Points* contained in this book were designed specifically for that very purpose, and you will find that, taken together, they form a solid foundation upon which you can begin to hone your craft and greatly improve your storytelling abilities. You can think of the seven *Points* as a fine-grained whetstone that, if adhered to, will give your writing a keen edge.

After you have completed the seven *Points* and have absorbed the various lessons within them, you can begin implementing the new methods in your writing, which, for one thing, will enable you to place yourself directly at the center of each scene in your story, where you essentially belong if you intend to successfully translate your vision to the page with forceful expression and to the delight of your readers.

At the end of each *Point* you will find a worksheet that ties in directly to the particular *Point* that precedes it. By filling out these worksheets, you will be given in-depth information about your characters and enough fodder for as many interesting situations as you wish to place them in. Your characters will begin to have real purpose as they navigate the winding route of your plot, and the story itself will be rich with details that readers can readily absorb.

—DANIEL MIDDLETON

POINT 1

Understanding the Purpose of a Novel

THE BIG QUESTION

THE BIG QUESTION

TO BEGIN, I ask you, dear reader, "What is the purpose of a novel?" This is not necessarily related to another question, "Why have you decided to *write* a novel?" The second question can have various answers, many, if not all of them, involving some personal agenda on the part of the writer or writers in question. But the answer to the first question, and in all truth, there really is only one true answer (which many may debate), is to entertain. Let's face it: storytelling has always been a form of entertainment, well before books, movies, and television. People, since the dawn of time, have entertained one another with tales. The novel form was invented to continue this tradition and make it available to the masses.

Keeping in mind that a novel's main—and in most cases nowadays, *sole*—purpose is to entertain, a writer should be able to approach a book with this singular agenda in mind, abutting it and supplementing it with experimentation, lofty artistic objectives, or other personal goals, so long as the primary agenda remains in full frontal view. A lot of writers, when setting out to write a magnum opus of some kind, or the *Great American Novel*, lose sight of this singular agenda, placing everything before it, thus leaving their readers scratching their heads at the ridiculousness they've been mercilessly beset by.

During my brief stint as an anonymous blogger, I dedicated what little time I could spare from my career duties to review books published by mostly amateur writers, usually via print-on-demand. During this time, I happened to criticize one writer for having published a few stories that were absolutely vapid and lacking plots. His best and only defense was that James Joyce was more or less accused of similar literary crimes—particularly those that concern stories without plots. This could have led to a lot of heavy-handed rebuttals on my part, but I decided to digress, because I had no intention of belittling struggling writers, as it is neither my desire nor place to.

I said that to say this: Joyce, Faulkner, Nabokov, Pynchon . . . contemporary writers can use them as an excuse to apply their own brand of experimentation to literature all they want—as though these souls, by so doing, gave contemporary authors license to do so as well—but bear in mind that all of them experimented in various novels with the goal of entertaining their readers. And I believe all of them succeeded.

All of the aforementioned authors understood story dynamics, character, and language; they attempted to make every detail of their narratives interesting, despite the sometimes mundane nature of the action being described. James Joyce's books, for instance, contain many passages that are pumped full with lyrical prose and vivid imagery, even with terse clauses and seeming half-phrases applied. This is not to say that these writers will appeal to everyone. I raise the point simply to say that, given their skill and despite their experimentation, each of them managed to write at such a high level that their material was vastly entertaining to a certain class of readers, while those whose literary predilections led them in a different direction could appreciate their great abilities. That said, while none of these writers are among my favorites, I also admire their literary skill and have to point out that their books are still being discovered and enjoyed by a new generation of readers today!

As regards the topic of entertainment, I understand that what might be entertaining to one reader may not be so to another, but good literature is good literature, and the majority among us can agree on what constitutes a bad book. And when I use the word "entertain" I'm basically implying that your story must be written in a way that it not only grabs hold of your readers but also keeps them flipping the pages. That is not to say that you have to write a suspense novel or action-thriller, you simply have to write enthralling material, despite the genre. To give you an example, I am equally enthralled by Dashiell Hammett's *The Maltese Falcon* as I am by Pearl S. Buck's *The Good Earth*, and these books operate in two totally different arenas. It doesn't take action and suspense to enthrall a reader; it takes powerful storytelling, whether that story involves an outlaw being hunted by government forces armed to the teeth, or an old Chinese woman bent on reaping a vast harvest on her own despite the sudden death of her farmer husband.

Bear this in mind: aside from the occasional school assignment, religious study, or other like purpose, the attraction we hold for books in general is based, foremost, on the fact that we view them as a source of enjoyment. In addition to the usual reasons offered by some—you know, the pursuit of intellectual stimulation or growth; spiritual enlightenment, what have you—people mainly read fiction to be entertained.

We want to be swept into a story—be absorbed by it, if you will—by the sheer elements involved. We want to be drawn in by compelling characters, be they rogues or savants, jaded spinsters or ruthless businessmen, or valiant warriors. And even if it's a self-help book or lengthy exposition of nanotechnology, the information has to be presented in a manner that is conducive to holding our interest—meaning it has to entertain in some way.

Your Foundational Purpose

What I'm attempting to do here is get you to wrap your mind around the main objective of storytelling, so that you will understand your foundational purpose as you work toward bringing whatever vision you have in mind to life. If you forget that your main purpose is to entertain your readers, then you may become engrossed in aspects of your story that defy the conventions of the novel form, resulting in the alienation of your readership.

What's more, writing a novel should be fun, and so should reading one. Granted, it will take a great deal of work on the part of the writer, but the actual process of crafting the story itself should be fun and rewarding. If you are writing something that is completely burdensome to you, especially with regard to subject matter you're not thoroughly familiar with, the average reader will immediately pick up on that, as passages will be laden with unnecessary information and complex descriptions that do not allow for easy absorption.

My philosophy is this: if the material your story is concerned with is of great interest to you, and you're really passionate about it, and you place the same passion you have for whatever subject you're intent on chronicling into your writing, this will be transmitted to any reader with a proclivity for that type of material; they will be as infected by it as you were when you were writing about it.

You've heard the old saying: "Write what you know." Whether you believe or adhere to that or not, or how you interpret it is your concern. But my advice is this: you should write from a place of experience. If you long to write in a genre that you love to read but have never attempted to write, then do so by injecting personal experiences into the narrative; infuse those experiences into the characters and situations. Write from a place of experience. Simple as that. We have all experienced things via hobbies, vacations, excursions—the list is infinite. If you're writing a fantasy novel and you love sailing, send your characters

BONUS POINT

Recognize your strengths and exploit them; identify your weaknesses and avoid them on a voyage that will set your hair on fire as you write the scene. Say you're not familiar with medieval terminology; it's not your strength. Don't rely heavily on this.

Do your research, learn what terms were used for what (the names of swords, the ranks of knights and castle servants, etc.) but stick to your guns. Don't try to write like George R. R. Martin when it comes to chronicling medieval times. You can write in any genre if your narrative is infused with material that is written from a place of experience. You love adventure? Well and fine. Write through the eyes of a boy with an adventurous spirit. Since he is a boy, he doesn't have to understand the particulars of his medieval world in every detail. He's a boy! Readers won't expect him to know the king's business on any intimate level. But he might sneak around the castle grounds and overhear conversations that can be formed from your research. Then take him back on an adventurous journey away from all that and show us things you've experienced: exotic lands, the joy derived from discovering the hidden beauty of a foreign culture, what have you (of course you'll throw this in amidst some kind of plot that involves traditional fantasy themes). Lovers of fantasy fiction will be able to enjoy a fantasy epic from your point of view, with your particular spin on it. And this is true for any genre you choose to write in.

How a Novel Fulfills its Purpose

The simple fact is, people are entertained by novels mainly because, through them, they are allowed to enjoy vicarious thrills and experiences. Many people will actually "live," in a sense, through fictional characters and situations. Therefore, you have to allow for this by filling the pages of your book with things you've experienced firsthand. Please note the definition of the word "vicarious," which is taken from *The American Heritage Dictionary of the English Language: Fourth Edition*:

1. Felt or undergone as if one were taking part in the experience or feelings of another.
2. Endured or done by one person substituting for another.
3a. Acting or serving in place of someone or something else; substituted.

Take a look at the first sense: "Felt or undergone as if one were taking part in the ***experience*** or ***feelings*** of another." In other words, your readers are supposed to feel or undergo things in your novel and take part in them through your characters. How can you properly convey those experiences or feelings via characters and situations if you have not truly experienced them firsthand? It is nigh impossible. No one's imagination runs that deep. You have to really dive a coral reef in order to powerfully convey that particular experience through your writing. Researching the marine life that is found there is one thing; describing the feelings that are derived from the actual experience is quite another.

Even someone who is not a writer can more powerfully convey what they felt when they experienced a robbery firsthand than an experienced writer who has never been robbed! Say you love skydiving, but you weren't always free of a fear of heights; well, you have a compelling character arc right at your fingertips. (We'll go into the subject of character arcs and character building in greater detail in *Point Four*.)

Put another way, people love to live vicariously through the experiences of others. But nothing allows for that better than a novel (though film, television, theater, and other forms of entertainment run a close second, in my opinion). A novel gives a reader direct access into the minds of the characters depicted, be they womanizers or alcoholics or victims of abuse. Have you ever been a womanizer? Are you a recovering alcoholic? Have you ever experienced any kind of abuse in your life? My word! You could churn out rich material at the stroke of a pen by channeling whatever pain or suffering you've experienced, while others would have to spend months researching the things you're already bottling up. Be reminded that your personal experiences should be your primary literary strength, as no one else can chronicle those experiences as accurately and effectively as you can. Even the books I mentioned above, which were written by Hammett and Buck, were written from places of experience. Dashiell Hammett had been a private detective in real life, and Pearl S. Buck, an American novelist, actually lived in China for most of her life. They both infused their material with personal experiences, which lifted their writing to another level, giving it immense power.

Writing from a place of experience is extremely critical in creating impacting moments; and really, all you want to do is string a long series of impacting moments together to form your story. In essence, each scene you write should result in a delightful vicarious experience for the reader. They shouldn't feel like they have to breeze through one scene in order to get to more exciting or stimulating aspects of your story. To keep your readers riveted, you have to completely inhabit each scene you write, even if it involves two people sitting in a living room conversing over drinks. Your goal is to make that conversation something worthy of taking part in, and remember that this is one of the goals of your novel: to allow the reader to take part in the experience of your characters.

You're not going to reach into your bag of experiences and pull out something mundane; the conversation, as I said, has to be worthy of our time; it also has to make us *want* to be a part of it. Plotting your book in a way that will force you to place two characters in a room to have a conversation that contains elements you yourself have never experienced, or that includes things you've never fully invested in, will result in weak, stilted, and forgettable material.

If you can avoid it, try not to fit things you haven't experienced into a plot. Fit your plot to your experiences. That is one of the secrets to creating a powerful narrative. And that is one way to keep your readers entertained!

Worksheet 1

WHAT ARE MY FIVE PRIMARY OBJECTIVES FOR THIS NOVEL?
(The fewer words you use, the better.)

1. ______
2. ______
3. ______
4. ______
5. ______

WHO WILL CONSTITUTE MY GENERAL READERSHIP?
(e.g., mystery readers, coin collectors)

1. ______
2. ______
3. ______
4. ______
5. ______

(Remember to keep them in mind when writing your novel.)

IN A SINGLE PARAGRAPH, DETAIL YOUR LITERARY STRENGTHS.

DESCRIBE YOUR LITERARY WEAKNESSES.
(This may also be based on criticism from others.)

LIST YOUR MOST INTERESTING EXPERIENCES BELOW, AND APPLY THEM EITHER TO A CHARACTER OR A SITUATION YOU WOULD PLACE A CHARACTER IN, AND WRITE EITHER A "C" OR AN "S" NEXT TO EACH CHOICE.
(e.g., Backpacking in Europe "S"; Fly Fishing "C"; Mountain Climbing "S"; Gardening "C")

POINT 2

Drawing Inspiration

BUILD ON WHAT CAME BEFORE

BUILD ON WHAT CAME BEFORE

I REALIZE THAT, DESPITE A WRITER'S LOVE for the novel form, and writing itself for that matter, moments of inspiration come and go, and authors are sometimes left in a murky creative pool. This *Point* will proffer a few novel means of literary inspiration that I hope will not only aid in offsetting those moments but also allow writers to take home a few creative lessons.

Before you even attempt to write a book, you should have some concept of what kind of story you want to tell, and the best way to capture a future tale is to build on previous ones that have been told in the past. A wise man once said that there is nothing new under the sun. That goes for novels as well. All stories that will be conceived by tomorrow's writers have already been told at least once. The joy in "retelling" a tale (and that is what all books, movies, TV shows, and plays do nowadays) is telling it in a new way. That is what you have to do. Rather than wracking your brain in an attempt to come up with something completely original (an impossibility, let me tell you now), you should simply chart a creative course to familiar narrative waters. That is what James Cameron did when he retold *Pocahontas* as *Avatar*, essentially setting it in space and tossing in an alien race to shake things up a bit.

Let's put it this way: all great stories, be they delivered in the form of plays, movies, video games, comic books, television shows, what have you, were inspired by something that came before. Many creators and writers of successfully repackaged stories will tell you, quite frankly, that they drew inspiration for their story from some kind of source material. George Lucas did it with *Star Wars*, as he drew heavily from Joseph Campbell's book on mythology, *The Hero With a Thousand Faces*, a book that shares essential story elements and overall direction with Lucas's space saga. Of note, Campbell himself believed that all stories have already been told, and I, as you already know, agree wholeheartedly.

Lucas, as it is widely known, also borrowed from Akira Kurosawa's *Hidden Fortress* (1958), *Sanjiro* (1962), and *Yojimbo* (1961), infusing many of the beloved characters in *Star Wars* with characteristics from the peasants and samurais that peopled Kurosawa's films (and samurai swords became lightsabers). The borrowing did not start there, however, for Kurosawa himself drew from American Westerns and detective stories, particularly Dashiell Hammett's first novel, *Red Harvest* (1928), which was a major inspiration for *Yojimbo.*

I hope you see where I'm going. For many generations, great writers have been building on the work of their predecessors. Note the operative word in the previous sentence, *building*, in the sense that successive generations of great writers often improve on what came before, thus taking the tales of yesterday to a higher level. We see this with the acclaimed succession of the three greatest detective novelists that ever lived (or wrote in this case), namely Hammett, who is credited with inventing the modern crime novel; Chandler, who improved on Hammett's work by polishing the prose of his books to such a degree that the atmospheric and lyrical language is now arguably regarded as literature; and Ross MacDonald, who achieved the unthinkable by building on the great Raymond Chandler by adding a psychological depth to the detective novel that is perhaps still unmatched today.

Again, since there is no new thing under the sun, no story that will ever be told will be completely and one hundred percent original, no matter what. What is of greatest importance here is this: it is always good to build a story or a series or anything you intend to write on something that preexisted. Not that you're going to copy what came before, mind you. I am in no way suggesting that you plagiarize the material of others. What I want you to understand is that drawing inspiration from source material makes for easier and smoother storytelling, in that a source acts as a wonderful reference point, which your story can center around. Rather than straining your mind in a feeble attempt to create something that no one else has ever envisioned, you should look to something that already exists. Study that property, and, most importantly, find ways to improve upon it. Inventors do this all the time. Everything we see around us evolved from something that came before it. No inventor invents a thing from thin air without building or improving on something that was conceived prior to their invention. Stories are no different. Even if you think that no one else has thought of your story idea, you can be sure that it exists in one archaic form or another.

This should not dissuade or discourage you in any way. In fact, a writer should take heart and apply what is being said here in their own writing. You see, by drawing on a source and infusing ideas and story elements from that source into your own tale, you will deliver something familiar to your intended readership. In essence, your readers will have something to go on when they read your story. In other words, familiar elements in your tale will allow them to access whatever it is you're trying to say in a new way. They won't feel alienated because they can't identify with some weird, illogical world you've created, which has no bearing on anything that has been seen or experienced before. Readers like to identify with the familiar, albeit in new and improved ways. That is why we tend to revisit proven genres over and over again. And if a new subgenre is introduced, it has to be delivered in a way that breeds familiarity. If we're talking about a tale of space aliens, we still want to see war, redemption, romance, or heroic feats of derring-do—in other words, familiar story elements. Readers need something to anchor their emotions to. They need to pine for two ill-fated lovers to unite in some unforgettable way, despite the odds against them (even if those lovers are CGI aliens or robots or cartoon characters). You see, familiarity is key in all of this, and storytellers of the past have long set the rules; rules that we as readers and moviegoers respect. We need conflict and resolution. We need to see character arcs: antagonists experiencing a change of heart after an amazing series of events alters their course. We need to see people lose heart, and successful people fail; on the other hand, we need to see failures succeed. In other words, we want familiarity; things that we as human beings living in a real world can identify with, even though we're looking for escapism. And the best way to deliver that familiarity is to take dynamic and essential elements from a preexisting tale (or tales) and repackage them. Simple as that. All of the great writers have done and continue to do this. But you must do so consciously and with expertise, taking care not to plagiarize. The idea is to pay homage to the work of others, or better yet, make allusions to their works.

So if you have a tale in mind that inspires you . . . if you've watched a great film, or you've read a sensational novel, draw inspiration from this. We've all been touched by offerings from great filmmakers, playwrights, and writers, and they, in turn, have been touched by amazing storytellers that came before them. You as a writer need to take up the torch and build on what they have done. You need to look at their work and say, "Hey, I would love to do that, but in my own way. I could take it in a different direction." That is how subgenres are created. One writer, inspired by another, decides to take a collection of story elements and put his or her own spin on it, so much so that it forces the creation of a new genre. The detective novel experienced this as it evolved from the Agatha Christie cozies and Victorian world of Sherlock Holmes to Hammett and Chandler's bleak and more deadly PI worlds, where everyone seemed jaded or cynical. Today, the genre has evolved even further, giving us the police procedural and the medical thriller, among other subgenres.

So you as a writer should feel free to take what has gone before and put a new spin on it. That is how inspiration generally works. The world is your oyster. In short, inspiration is a writer's fuel, and bookstores, libraries, movie theaters, and television are your filling stations.

Bonus Point

The quality of the work that inspires you will determine the quality of your writing. So fill up on high-octane

TV or Not TV

Granted, while you're looking at a series of books from accomplished authors, you'll probably become a little intimidated, seeing these are finished products, with worlds and characters that are fully realized, while yours are still at a nascent stage. You may be thinking of writing a seven-book series and are looking at the works of writers who have done the same. This is probably not a good idea. Why? Because they've put in a tremendous amount of work, conducted an enormous amount of research, and spent perhaps many years writing their seven-volume tome. This can prove too daunting for an untested writer who is just sliding his or her toe up to the starting line of a new novel. I propose something else.

While it is a different creative medium altogether, I find that television—good television—can be an effective purveyor of important literary lessons. In fact, I'll go as far as to say that drawing inspiring from a creative medium *other* than the one you are currently working in is probably best. I know of many writers who read books by authors they hope to somehow emulate, albeit in a small way, only to come away dissatisfied because they couldn't quite capture the essence of what their admired author seemed to convey so effortlessly. By watching a good television program, however, and gleaning insights into effective and forceful portrayals of human behavior, one can transfer those lessons onto paper without the undo pressure of trying to live up to the lofty standards of a literary predecessor.

This is not meant to contradict my advice to one writer, however, to whom I said: "If you want to write well, read as much as you can. Devour anything and everything that inspires you. Learn from the greats." By reading a good amount of quality literature—that is, books that are put together well, written well, edited thoroughly, and so on—a writer can learn how language is to flow on paper, where punctuations are supposed to fall; how sentences, dialogue, and narrative on a whole is to be constructed. But when it comes to drawing inspiration, most writers who pick up a good book with this in mind will either become despondent when they realize that they cannot successfully capture the magic of the author they admire, or else they will attempt to copy an admired writer's style, language, or story, to their detriment. This is why I suggest creative mediums other than your own as the best sources of inspiration.

The reason I suggest television as an alternate medium for inspiration, and not film, is this: the average television show, particularly an hour-long drama, has roughly 22 episodes to a season, which is very similar to the makeup of a novel—each episode acting as a chapter of a book, and the season being the book. It would take roughly 16.5 hours to devour a full season of a dramatic series (sans the commercials)—the rough equivalent of the time it would take a person, reading at a normal pace, to complete a full-length novel. Over the course of that 22-episode season, characters would go through various changes—including ups and downs and the inevitable arcs—and we would see character flaws develop in some and virtues develop in others. I can't think of a better source of inspiration than the medium of television for someone who is stuck in a creative slump.

As far as choices go, there is something out there for just about everyone. For those who are given to character-driven stories, I'd say, for instance, take a look at *Six Feet Under*. (It's time to put that Netflix account to good use.) By watching a mere season of this show, one can learn a great deal about character interaction and development and how to create personality nuances that will allow your readers to interpret subtle variations in your characters. And for those who are given to plot-driven stories, I'd say consider ABC's *Lost*, which not only demonstrates the use of crucial plot devices, timing, and atmosphere but also serves as a good model in the department of character development, given its clever and carefully woven backstories. But feel free to pick and choose what you will, as long as it inspires you and gets your creative juices flowing.

Bear in mind that one would, at the very least, have to rely heavily on intuition for what I'm proposing here, as many of these lessons won't be apparent to the casual observer. A serious writer, however, will spot them for sure.

I'm not suggesting that you simply pick a show, grab a snack and a drink, kick your feet up, and tune your brain out as you enjoy your favorite hour-long drama. Far be it from me to imply any such thing. What I'm suggesting is that you keenly study the program of your choice and imbibe its many lessons like fine wine. But you have to pick your show of choice wisely, because not all television dramas offer rich characters, story, and plot.

Music to Write By

Kerouac is said to have written his masterpiece, *On the Road*, in a mere three weeks, on a single roll of telegraph paper at that, so he wouldn't have to interrupt his flow by the obligatory act of changing paper. Beat legend has it that he wrote the book while seated at a kitchen table in his apartment on West 20th Street right here in New York, in a spontaneous, surrealistic free-flow that was propelled by pea soup, coffee, and yes, lots of Benzedrine. What resulted is a book that became an important fixture in American literature. My former mentor introduced me to Kerouac by having me read that book, and a new world was immediately opened to me. It's one that I have never left.

Raymond Chandler, on the other hand—among my favorite writers of all time—is said to have written the Oscar-nominated screenplay for *The Blue Dahlia* in a haze of drunkenness and would often be found passed out at his table. The film turned out all right, but for a film noir entry it pales in comparison to far superior efforts, such as Jacques Tourneur's *Out of the Past*—hands down, my favorite noir. (I could go on about classic films forever.) Chandler's novels are quite another matter, however, as those have gone down in history as important hard-boiled fare, in effect both broadening the scope of the genre and cementing it—written under the influence or not.

There are many other stories one could relate about writers who relied on one form of substance or another to fuel their creativity, but I'll leave those to you. Rather than rely on drugs and alcohol, however, writers could derive inspiration from far less abusive mediums. One that interests me most is music. Though he was a religious skeptic, the late, great Kurt Vonnegut wrote in his final collection of essays, *A Man Without a Country*, that "if I should ever die, God forbid, let this be my epitaph: 'The only proof he needed for the existence of God was music.' " He also claimed that music aided him during times of tragedy.

I don't think there needs to be a treatise on the benefits and effects of music (effects both ill and good); we are all of us familiar with its power, having fallen under it at one point or another in our lives. And as far as the entertainment industry is concerned—be it theater, anything associated with the nightlife, and even film and television—music is as much a staple as the very people involved. Try to imagine a film without a score or a television program that opens or closes without a theme song (well, nowadays, there's probably just such a thing). Music is integral when it comes to any form of entertainment. I think this should apply even at the inception of your creative work—your novel—from the concept stage. Beyond that, a choice song might inspire you to get past that rough patch in your story, or to visualize a scene more fully; it might help you to beef up the tension or highlight the conflict in your book; but barring all of that, it may very well just set you in the mood to write, giving you the proper state of mind and what have you, after which you can cut the power on your CD player.

I remember watching Turner Classic Movies a few years back, and they were running a promo for their *31 Days of Oscar*, where they featured a slew of films that won (or I believe were nominated for) Academy Awards. It was probably a thirty-second spot, but it was quite effective. And the one reason I responded so positively to it was because of that hypnotic contemporary song that played in the background against images of Bette Davis, Cary Grant, Joan Crawford, Katherine Hepburn, Clark Gable, Humphrey Bogart, and so many others, moving in striking achromatic brilliance. I watched the month-long tribute to the Oscar-worthy classics, even though I'd seen many of the films before. That is how powerful the promo was, how effective—and all because of the song, working in unison with the unforgettable moving images of Tinsel Town's finest. And like the lyrics from that song—*Daylight Robbery*, performed by Essex native Imogen Heap—when I think back on those films and that promo, "it gets me right here . . . every time."

Worksheet 2

List Five TV Shows That Closely Relate to the Book You will Write.
(Study these shows while writing your story.)

1. ______
2. ______
3. ______
4. ______
5. ______

(Pay close attention to plot points, character and story arcs, and narrative flow.)

List Five Music Artists You Find Most Inspiring.
(Compile an MP3 playlist of their best songs.)

1. ______
2. ______
3. ______
4. ______
5. ______

(Listen to them to inspire key scenes in your story as you write.)

Briefly Describe the Most Inspiring Story You've Read or Movie You've Watched.
(But one that will influence your own story. This may be from childhood or a more recent experience.)

List 15 Story Elements or Themes That Stood Out Most.
(e.g., "Bravery," "A heightened sense of danger," "Self-sacrifice," etc.
And consider similar story elements and themes for your own story.)

Point 3

Finding Your Voice

LITERARY VOICES

LITERARY VOICES

I KNOW MANY OF YOU HAVE YOUR favorites when it comes to established authors. I have my own, of course. One thing is certain, though, of the many beloved authors out there, quite a few of them have garnered the large followings they currently enjoy because of their exceptional skill at delivering tales, whether entirely fictional or not. If you can't deliver a good story, your career is pretty much cooked (even some authors who can deliver the goods have a hard time catching on, for various reasons).

I think it is obvious by now that I am drawn to a good story, whether that story is riddled with grammatical errors or written by a hand that isn't so deft. A good story is a good story, and I have heard my share of them, first from my father, who recounted tales of his youth with a certain candid quality, all of which enthralled me, and then from others in my family. Books came last on a long list of sources, but I have delighted in and been swept into numerous tales since I began reading many years ago.

For me, what makes a story really resonate is the way in which it is told, and I am referring mainly to the author's prose style. I am drawn to good prose like a shark to blood, if I must paint a picture. I like to see sentences written in a way that I have never seen them written before, but with fluidity, and sans any well-worn figures of speech. I like vivid descriptions of people and places and things, and the writing could either be chiefly ornate or rhythmic, so long as it fits the story, or better yet, the genre. For instance, James Joyce's prose style wouldn't work in a hardboiled novel, but you know that.

One thing an author needs to establish him- or herself in the literary arena, and thus attract a following, is a unique voice, and a consistent one if he or she can manage it. Any good and dedicated author will eventually, by way of accident or design, acquire a voice, a literary style that is unique to him or her, and by which that author can be readily identified by their current flock of readers. That voice will also be the signature of that author—his or her distinctive characteristic or mark, if you will—which a reader will come to expect. For instance, after reading one Raymond Chandler book, realizing that his was a voice unique to him—a voice that I found refreshing and appealing—I didn't bother to read the blurbs or reviews of his books anymore, but bought them on spec, partly knowing what I was in for based solely on the author's voice. The same goes for Kerouac, Fitzgerald, Hammett, and even many contemporaries.

The reclusive J. D. Salinger, though he published one book and too few short stories and novellas, displayed a unique and timeless voice himself. With Salinger in mind, the one thing that has to be associated with your voice is theme. Recurring themes must accompany your tales; themes that readers will view as little threads running through all your works, as we will also come to expect these things. Chandler had them, Kerouac had them, Hammett had them, and Salinger certainly had them. These themes can involve bravery, friendship, betrayal, redemption, abandonment, or anything you desire or can identify with, so long as it is executed well. A theme is best delivered when it is something you strongly identify with or believe in (again, write from a place of experience).

I know that some of you writers out there like to experiment, and some of you will even attempt to write a new unexplored work each time you publish, but bear this in mind: you will attract a different set of readers with each of those works. Writing with a distinctive voice, however, and offering recurring themes in your various works will not cause you to alienate your current fan base. If readers really respond to your writing in one novel, why abandon them by jettisoning everything that made that book work? If you *must* experiment, however, do so under a pen name or names, like every wise writer who has navigated that path before you. But continue writing your signature material under one name. That way everyone wins.

Be Yourself

One important fact to consider is that all writers who have locked onto a distinctive literary voice have achieved this by doing one thing: being who they are. Your literary voice is just that, *your* literary voice, and no one else's. Just as no one can write with your distinctive literary signature, neither can you write with another author's particular literary lilt. Mark Twain, who currently holds the distinction of having possessed the most notable and well-known literary voice in America and perhaps the world, wrote his stories by tapping into past experiences gained from a rugged frontier life that was peppered with the Southern tradition. He embraced that life, transferring much of it onto paper in a colloquial style that was as familiar to him as your lifestyle is to you. Therefore, you need to do likewise. Do not try to emulate Henry James or Jane Austen if you grew up in Louisiana and have never left. I wager that if you were to tap into your past and embrace the lifestyle that you have known all your life, a full-bodied narrative complete with a rich tapestry of characters awaits. And if you delivered that narrative in your own style, with your own particular way of speaking, thinking, and rationalizing, a unique literary voice would emerge that you could call your very own.

Bonus Point

Literary voices are like DNA, each writer possesses the ability to express their own

Stream of Consciousness

As defined by Wikipedia, stream of consciousness "is the continuous flow of sense-perceptions, thoughts, feelings, and memories in the human mind or a literary method of representing a blending of mental processes in fictional characters, usually in an unpunctuated or disjointed form of interior monologue." Put another, looser, way, a writer can go wild on paper and write whatever comes to mind without restriction. Virginia Woolf was notorious for applying the stream of consciousness narrative mode in her works, as were Kerouac and Faulkner, and William Styron even got into the mix.

I am not suggesting that you undertake the task of writing an entire novel in a stream of consciousness free flow. This would require a great deal of study, first and foremost. What I am suggesting is that you sit down and write something fictional, directly from the heart in one complete burst, in a kind of stream of consciousness free flow. Don't ponder on it too long or break for air, just write, write, write. Pretty much whatever comes to mind. Refrain from reaching for a dictionary and resist the urge to Google facts or locations. The idea is to write an authentic piece of fiction in the voice that is your very own. And while doing so, you should draw on memories and snatches of the past. And feel free to tap into your deepest desires—explore them—and live out your fantasies on paper.

Do this as many times as you like, creating a series of flash fiction pieces that can be as short as 500 or 1,000 words in length. With enough practice, and a sizeable collection of stream of consciousness shorts under your belt, you should begin to tap into your unique narrative voice. And when writing actual fiction that you intend to publish or circulate, you will find it very easy to call on your voice at will. It will flow from you as naturally as actual speech itself.

Worksheet 3

List Five of the Most Unique Voices in Literature You can Recall.
(Either fiction or nonfiction writers will do.)

1. __________
2. __________
3. __________
4. __________
5. __________

(They don't have to be great writers, just memorable ones.)

List Five of the Most Important Things in Your Life.
(These should speak to who you are.)

1. __________
2. __________
3. __________
4. __________
5. __________

(It can be music, food, dating, cars, or one single thing with various layers.)

Using the Five Important Things You Listed, Describe a Fictional Character Below.
(This is a protagonist based on you, who will star in your first stream of consciousness flash fiction piece.)

List 15 Story Titles Below at Random.
(These can be anything that comes to mind, and they can range from the ridiculous to the profound, but be reminded that you will eventually write a flash fiction stream of consciousness piece for each one.)

POINT 4

Establishing Your Main Character

Creating Your Main Character

Creating Your Main Character

As readers, when we crack open a work of fiction, we do so with the hope that we will embark on a journey that will thrill and captivate us and cause us to identify with, or at least embrace, the purpose and drive of the main character. It is your protagonist, after all, who is the captain of your literary ship, and it is he or she who will carry us through the story. That protagonist, therefore, had better be as interesting as they come. And as real as they come.

The best protagonists are the ones that are drawn from one's own personal experiences. It goes without saying that being able to tap into the deep well of one's own past is invaluable for a writer. Once you imbue this lead character with your own emotional traits, your own passions and leanings, you in effect inject that character with pieces of yourself. What results is a protagonist with which many readers can identify, as we are all cut from the same cloth. Through the fictional journey of your protagonist, you can elicit any emotional response you desire from your readers, depending on what it is you decide to inject into your lead.

As you consider your main character, think about the sweeping narrative you will thrust them in, and settle on your major arc from the outset. Does the character start out poor only to end up rich? Or are they insecure, self-conscious, and reserved at the start of your novel and confident and self-assured by the end? These are things you must know going in. It will allow you to season the character with the right emotions and mindset based on appropriate periods in your own life. If the character starts out poor, for instance, you'll have to recall a time in your own life where you were without enough means, despite your best efforts to the contrary. Draw on the feelings that coursed through you at that time, the fear and worry, the dread of probably never being able to stick your head above water again. Inject all of that into your character and build your plot around it. Let your own experiences guide your character's journey, not to the point of an autobiography, of course; you're simply going to gather the choicest parts of your life for the sake of your character. You want to breathe life into them after all, and what better way to do that than to apply things you've seen and experienced firsthand: the feelings you actually felt, disappointments that have crushed you, decisions that once weighed heavily upon you?

When creating your main character, don't try to add flavoring you think will appeal to the masses. If your aim is to please everyone, you'll fail miserably each and every time. Instead, seek only to capture the very essence of your character, and convey whatever message your overall story will carry through his or her thoughts, actions, and reactions. Figure out what it is you want this character to say, and I'm not referring to dialogue, I'm talking about the overall theme of your book, its core message, be it redemption, forgiveness, justice, or whatever powerful moral you want your readers to carry with them.

CONSISTENCY AND CHARACTER ARCS

Consistency is important when it comes to character portrayal. Speech patterns need to be locked down and personalities honed through consistent narrative tailoring, and, following this, the protagonist should never slip *out of character*, so to speak. When certain turns of phrases have been locked in and descriptive mannerisms defined, the character begins to settle in the reader's mind; they begin to grow comfortable with the personality you've created, but they can only do so if the character seems real enough to them. Just because you're writing fiction doesn't mean you're not going to imbue your characters with real personalities. That's where personal experience comes in, even if your main character is based largely on someone other than yourself. And that is something that tends to happen with writers; personalities of people who have made an impression in your life will often seep into your characters, and that is a good way to approach *Point Five*, which we will come to in the next chapter. You can do a little of this with your protagonist as well. After all, in many cases, it may not be a good idea to base a lead character entirely on yourself if you intend for that character to live things out that you never truly experienced firsthand. For instance, you might want to write a sea epic but have only been on a couple of cruises. However, you have an uncle who was in the Navy during time of war. Your protagonist, therefore, can exist with that in mind, being based largely on your uncle, who you will interview to no end—but again, your book will not be written to the point of a biography.

Once you have a view of your main character, right down to personality, mannerisms, speech patterns, and so on, you can start to create them by placing them in situations that are somewhat familiar to you. So while the character is based primarily on someone else, they will start out in a familiar situation, one that you can recount with ease. That way you can work your way up to more complex experiences outside of your own while getting to know the character intimately. So, if your book starts out on the open sea or in the midst of a major battle, you might want to hold off on writing that scene until you've learned your character inside out. Plot out the scene and come back to it later. The first scene you write should be fairly simple; perhaps one

Bonus Point

A book does not have to be written in chapter order. Start with the easiest parts and work your way around that starts out with one of your own experiences. It can be as simple as a conversation in bed with a spouse, which can be drawn from your own past. The character might express his fear about an unknown future or something else that has deeply affected you. Then other scenes can be worked in, such as the first conversation with the Navy recruiter, which you can flavor with echoes of past job interviews and your awkward reactions to questions posed or your confidence under pressure, whichever holds true.

Knowing the end from the beginning will help you ground your character as well. What I mean by this is that if you plan to have them end up rich but start out poor, their attitude has to reflect this; bitterness and resentment should be tamped down as the story progresses, but at carefully marked intervals that coincide with the narrative. If we take the proposed sea epic, for instance, we would want to explore something in your main character at the beginning of your story that will eventually shift in an entirely new direction, thus creating a character arc. Your Navy man might express a certain fear of the unknown while in bed with his wife, and he probably cites reasons for this. Perhaps as a child he saw his father succumb to a terrible illness that was the result of a grueling job, like coal mining. Naturally he fears he'll share the same fate, because his father was the sum total of his view of the working man. But the Navy opens him up to a world of new experiences, and he comes into contact with at least one character—a commanding officer or the like—who in effect acts as a father figure. This officer, unlike his real father, is a take-charge individual, striking out at life on his own terms. While emulating the officer, your main character will begin to embrace a new life with greater confidence, crushing his fear of the unknown even in the midst of a war, because the future, despite the present odds, is bright. And the horrors of war make him realize this, as does the experience and even-keeled nature of his commanding officer.

So while you want your characters to be consistent in manner, speech, and overall personality, you also have to account for major character arcs, which will show them in a new light as the arc unfolds. Consider your character arcs prior to writing your story, and make sure each is settled and established. The main purpose of the character arc is to alter the viewpoint of your protagonist via a series of events in the story. If he or she starts out one way, they will end up another upon the resolution of their personal journey. This is important to each and every narrative, but it doesn't necessarily have to conclude within one story. You can have the character arc play out across multiple stories or books. For instance, through 711 Press (www.711press.com), a publishing company I co-own with author and vocal coach Jaime Vendera, we publish what we call TV Books, which are episodic stories that comprise a full season, much like a traditional television show. Each season is roughly 13 episodes long, and character arcs are expressed over the course of a given season and sometimes extend through the show's entire run. One example is a TV Book we produced called *Mafiosi.*

The show starts out with Vincenzo Abruzzi, a young, out-of-work Italian-American male in 1950s New York who is approached by his cousin Paul after a neighborhood wise guy puts the word out that he needs to seed a few new spots. A chance meeting with this made man leads to a world of crime and excess after Vincenzo is given the chance to prove himself with a test run. Along the way, he meets both a nice Italian girl who could turn out to be wife material as well as a seasoned "woman of the world," who opens him up to new possibilities. Juggling these women while concentrating on furthering his criminal career without getting whacked by a slew of new enemies proves to be more difficult that it first seemed, but the allure of mob life is also too irresistible, especially when he begins to rise up the ranks with unprecedented speed. And it is this swift rise that causes our main character to go from a broke, unsure, and carefree individual to a seasoned, shrewd, and calculated businessman of sorts, and one that is extremely well-paid. But it is the various people he meets within the organization who shape his outlook the most. The main thing to consider here is that character arcs can work in any given situation and with any kind of character you can think up, so don't feel limited.

The Protagonist's Three Essentials

There are three essential things you must explore throughout your story concerning your protagonist, and all three must encompass your entire narrative. They are as follows:

1. What is your main character's goal (what are they after)?
2. What story elements will you use to prevent them from getting it?
3. How will they get around those story elements to achieve said goal?

The first question isn't necessarily one that the main character has to know the answer to at the outset of your story, nor is it one the reader has to know. But it is highly important that you, the writer, know up front. For instance, a story might start out with a main character who is so wrapped up in his daily routine, perhaps as a farmer, that he has no idea what wild adventures await him. Then a visitor stops by, a stranger by all accounts, but during the conversation this stranger seems to know more about our protagonist than meets the eye. Then we learn from this visitor that danger approaches, and before long our farmer must head out on a quest to find something or someone at all cost, since the fate of the world might hinge on this very thing or person. Of course, the first thing that prevents our supposed hero from venturing out might be himself. Reluctance might be our first answer to question 2. But once our hero does decide to embark on a quest you can hurl all sorts of obstacles at him, and you can raise the stakes with each one, until the final nail-biting one that might mean the end of our hero or the end of life on earth as we know it.

Once he figures out a way past this final obstacle, our story can come to an end. Some solutions may require the life of our hero, and some might lead us into a sequel, wherein we would rinse and repeat all three questions in a new adventure.

If you are a student of storytelling, you'll recognize these three questions in practically every play, movie, TV show, or book you've experienced, from *The Tale of the Allergist's Wife* to Showtime's *Dexter*. I urge that you study these questions carefully, look for them in your daily reading or viewing experience, and apply them in your storytelling.

Worksheet 4

LIST FIVE POSITIVE PERSONALITY TRAITS YOU FEEL YOU POSSESS.
(e.g., "inventive," "curious," "organized")

1. ______________________
2. ______________________
3. ______________________
4. ______________________
5. ______________________

(Think of these when sketching the main character in one of your stories.)

LIST FIVE NEGATIVE PERSONALITY TRAITS YOU FEEL YOU POSSESS.
(e.g., "nervous," "indifferent," "lazy")

1. ______________________
2. ______________________
3. ______________________
4. ______________________
5. ______________________

(Incorporate these traits into the personality of your main character and build on them.)

BRIEFLY DESCRIBE A PERSONAL AND MEMORABLE CHARACTER ARC YOU EXPERIENCED.
(This can be from any period of your life. Also explain what your original viewpoint was and what altered it.)

____

____

____

____

____

____

(Create a believable character arc for your main character by incorporating the same level of detail.)

LIST 5 MEMORABLE CHARACTERS BELOW. (Either from film or literature)	HOW DID THE CHARACTER START OUT? (e.g., "downtrodden," "shy")	HOW DID THE CHARACTER END UP? (e.g., "happy," "confident")
______________	______________	______________
______________	______________	______________
______________	______________	______________
______________	______________	______________
______________	______________	______________

Point 5

Rounding Out the Cast

MINOR CHARACTERS WITH MAJOR STORY FUNCTIONS

Minor Characters With Major Story Functions

While your full cast will be composed mainly of minor characters, they should in no way be minuscule literary figures to the point that they are forgettable. Each of your minor characters should have an important story function, and no two minor characters should function in the same capacity. If we're talking about military or police force, things of that nature, then they may have the same rank, but their story function should be unique—one might offer moral support to a main character while the other does the opposite.

That said, you should strike a balance when creating or fleshing out minor characters, as they shouldn't be allowed to take over your story or steal attention from the main characters. What you want to do is flavor your story broth with interesting characters, which will enrich the story itself and give it range, as well as an eclectic feel. You can introduce characters from far-flung regions or exotic lands, even if the main setting is the backwoods of Ohio. Whatever the case, your potential story range is limitless given the abundance of characters you can create.

One way to make a minor character stick in the minds of your readers is to create an interesting story entrance. Introduce them in a unique way or build up interest by mentioning them in dialogue beforehand. But when they are introduced, they should have a certain level of importance that is derived from their unique story function. In other words, how will they advance your plot? If your main character is accused of murder, don't just slide a run-of-the-mill defense attorney into the mix. Instead, have him be an antitype rather than an archetype. We remember characters that stand out by not towing the line, and we forget those who resemble every other bull in the herd.

I can recall a classic American Western titled *Shane* (1953) where Jack Palance, an actor who had trouble with horses, made a dramatic entrance as a villain by walking in with a horse rather than riding it. Because he led the horse on foot, this was seen as far more threatening than the planned gallop into town, which was dreadfully routine. Coming up with a unique introduction will not only cause your minor character to stand out but also help to shape and settle them into a unique personality.

Make Your Minors Stand Out

Names are extremely important, and in fiction the more unique a name the more it draws attention to the character and helps them stand out in the mind of the reader. But no two names should be so close that they cause confusion or diminish their individual impact. And while you wouldn't want your major characters to be too quirky or weird—unless that was your original intent (for example, Ignatius J. Reilly in the picaresque novel *A Confederacy of Dunces*)—your minor characters can be both. In fact, you might want them to be quirky, weird, and as unique as possible so long as they stand out and are remembered long after a reader closes the pages of your book.

You have to be careful not to overdo the names, however, as writers can easily get carried away with them. You have to come up with names that sound interesting, and if you can manage it, create names that will evoke a desired impression in the reader. Is your character menacing? Are they a precocious teenage girl? Is one of your minor characters a brainiac or a powerful wizard? Certain names can create instant impressions in the minds of readers, so choose them carefully.

Besides names, it is helpful to think of interesting or unique characteristics that will cause your minors to stand out; characteristics that might play a key role in your story as well. A character might be overweight, for instance, and their size might be used to intimidate an antagonist at some point. But the overweight issue might be played up in an interesting way that causes that characteristic to stand out even more. Perhaps the overweight character denies being overweight and considers him- or herself normal. He or she might never wear clothes that actually fit right. Or they might prefer to sit in chairs that are too small. There are many such scenarios you can come up with on your own that will fit in with your particular story. But whatever you do with your minor characters, make sure it isn't the norm, and that goes for speech patterns, mannerisms, physical descriptions, and general characteristics that make and define them. The last thing you want are minor characters that get lost in the background and do absolutely nothing for your story. In that case, they are better off not being introduced in the first place. Below you will note the description of a beloved minor character named Fiero, taken from a scene in a book released by 711 Press titled *The Crisis Artifact*:

> [Caesar's] thoughts were interrupted by a heavyset Ecuadorian leaning against a stretch limo that was parked in front of the tenement. With his arms still folded in front of him and a head of long, stringy black hair shaking from side to side, almost in disbelief he spoke to Caesar in Spanish, saying, *"El diablo en la carne!"*
>
> "Nice to see you, too, Fiero," Caesar replied.
>
> Considering his six-foot-tall stature, ferocious eyes, and a well-deserved reputation as one of Galton's attack [dog]s, Fiero seemed out of place as a chauffeur in the [snazz]y black suit he was wearing. Where his father-in-law

found his ruffians remained a mystery to Caesar, though over the years, Fiero had proved himself to be both a faithful employee and effective bodyguard.

You'll notice that the description of the character was laced within the story narrative itself and was offered with actions that showed us what he looked like rather than told us, which is what you want to do. He "shook" a stringy black head of hair, etc. To describe a character in great detail within two or three paragraphs—paragraphs that do nothing more than offer description—would only bombard the minds of your readers and offer them something to skip over. Instead, you want to lace clever character descriptions within scenes that actually advance the story. In the description above, we got a sense of the character's history as well as his looks and comportment.

BONUS POINT

Remember that anything you write has to add to your story, otherwise it's taking away from it

LOOK OUTSIDE YOURSELF FOR CHARACTER TYPES

As the title of this section suggests, you must look outside yourself for diverse character types. It's well and fine to pour yourself into the main character, or even one or two minor characters, but to really diversify your cast you must draw on others to create new molds. A good way to do this is to look to people you've associated with, particularly those who have made a deep impression in your life. It could be an uncle or a co-worker, a boss or ex flame. But you're only going to draw out the essence of that person and not recast them as a fictional character to the point of risking libel.

If you're in good standing with a relative, let's say, and they would be willing to provide fodder for your story or novel, perhaps you could record an interview that would yield interesting details you can work into your plot and characters. This is invaluable if you're considering writing on a subject you know very little about. And the person doesn't have to be close to you, they just have to be willing. A successful interview can lead to memorable, believable, and three-dimensional minor characters that can add an important dramatic function to your story.

Looking outside yourself means just that: you'll have to observe life as it happens around you. If you're sitting in a sidewalk restaurant, take notice of the people who pass you by. If you take advantage of public transportation, study your fellow passengers and look for interesting "tags," which are unique identifying character marks: hair style, eye color, body type, facial features, headgear, etc. By looking outside yourself and observing the people around you, minor characters will start to take shape in your mind, and you'll bring them to life with greater ease.

Worksheet 5

LIST FIVE MINOR CHARACTERS YOU INTEND TO USE IN A STORY.
(e.g., "cab driver," "ex-girlfriend," etc.)

1. ______
2. ______
3. ______
4. ______
5. ______

WHAT WILL BE THEIR PRIMARY STORY FUNCTION?
(e.g., "a shoulder to cry on")

1. ______
2. ______
3. ______
4. ______
5. ______

(Be as specific as possible.)

USING THE LINES BELOW, DESCRIBE SOMEONE IN YOUR LIFE WHO MIGHT PROVE TO BE AN INTERESTING MINOR CHARACTER IN YOUR STORY.

______

______

______

______

______

______

______

LIST 15 "TAGS" OR IDENTIFYING MARKS FOR MINOR CHARACTERS THAT WILL FIGURE IN A FLASH FICTION PIECE YOU WILL WRITE.
(e.g., "curly sideburns," "hawk nose," "extremely thin lips," "rakish smile," etc.)

______	______	______
______	______	______
______	______	______
______	______	______
______	______	______

POINT 6

Mastering Dialogue

ACTION AND REACTION

ACTION AND REACTION

DIALOGUE, IN SHORT, CAN BE the best conduit for conveying many things, if used correctly. It can impart vital information to your readership via a clueless character that is a stand-in for your readers, who will learn things as the reader does. It can heighten conflict and draw readers into that conflict as it is happening, which is more effective than narrative blocks that tell that same conflict. And it can create forward momentum for your story, keeping it flowing constantly forward, which is what you want to do in most cases. Essentially, dialogue is the only tool for creating fluid interaction and communication between your characters, in effect bringing them to life as only dialogue can.

One thing to understand concerning dialogue in novels is that characters shouldn't say something to one another just for the sake of saying it. When something is said, it should act as an action that requires a reaction. And action should precede reaction at all times, even in description that accompanies dialogue. If a character walks into a room that is already occupied, this will function as an action, to which people in the room will react, either by looking in his or her direction or reacting to a "Good morning, all." It is important that you create action/reaction scenarios in your dialogue exchanges and keep the order straight. Note that characters should not react before an action, but after. So you wouldn't write, "Baxter sat down. He felt tired," as that would convey a reaction/action to the reader. Rather, "Baxter felt tired, so he sat down," would be more appropriate, as Baxter is now reacting to the feeling or action of being tired. Dialogue should be treated in much the same way. One character acts, another reacts. And that should occur throughout all of your dialogue.

Say you have a scene where a boss arrives at the office, and his employees are already there, milling around. He can be an overbearing stuffed-shirt, but you don't have to tell that to your readers through narrative description. Bring your character to life by having him show that via good dialogue. Here you would use action/reaction to create tension, story momentum, and character development, all in one tiny scene that relies mainly on dialogue. For an example of this kind of effective dialogue, see the following scene, taken from a Season One episode of our TV Book *Mafiosi*:

> Once we loaded into the van, Tony Gallo explained the night's business. "We're pushin' straight through to Milwaukee, boys. Fourteen hours with our eyes open." That meant we would pull in around 2:00 a.m.
>
> Paul rode shotgun while I perched on the edge of a wooden crate just behind them. As we drove off I asked Tony Gallo a question. "Why Milwaukee? Pretty long trip for a heist, no?" ***(The dialogue here conveys important info to the reader in the form of a question. This is a reaction to the action from the first paragraph, where Tony Gallo explains the night's business. But Vincenzo's question, while a reaction to Tony Gallo's statement, also doubles as an action, to which the character Tony Gallo must now react. This is how dialogue should flow. Note that we also get a sense of where the action is taking place in preceding scene descriptions.)***
>
> "I hear ya, kid. We woulda hit their PA warehouse, 'cept the Philly crew out there got dibs on it. Milwaukee's

wide open, though. Virgin territory. Carlo's got real brains, you know? You two'll go places ridin' wid him." ***(Tony Gallo's reaction here conveys yet more info to the reader, though it is spoken to our main character, Vincenzo, who is new to this world. It would make no sense for Tony Gallo to explain these things to a seasoned veteran, as that character would already know all this. Writers tend to make the mistake of imparting info to the reader through two characters that are already aware of the things being said. This is a mistake.)***

"How long you been on his crew?" I asked. ***(New action.)***

"Now you're gettin' personal." ***(New reaction, and a somewhat unpleasant and unexpected one. We need the unexpected in dialogue. Things must be said that readers can't anticipate. This keeps things fresh. And here, Tony Gallo's personality is starting to shine through.)*** He glanced at me in the rearview mirror. "What's your name again?"

"Vincenzo," I said.

"A piece of advice, Vin—don't ask too much questions. This ain't therapy. You'll get yourself plugged doin' that." ***(This piece of dialogue not only adds to Tony Gallo's personality by showing us how he thinks but also colors the world we are navigating through as readers. It is a dangerous one, full of rules that could mean life or death.)***

"I try to tell him," Paul said.

"Try harder," Tony Gallo said. He didn't say anything else for the next few hours.

Note also that the dialogue tags are of the standard *said, asked* variety. You really don't need to get fancy where this is concerned. The simpler the better. We don't want to take attention away from what is being said by adding flourishes like "she admonished" or "he intoned." Using "said" and "asked" will suit your purpose.

Looking at the preceding dialogue we can see that a great deal was conveyed, and all of it "showed" rather than "told." We were right in the middle of the action as it unfolded. We know that this action took place inside a van, and it was around noon, judging from the time they would arrive in Milwaukee, where a supposed heist was scheduled. All dialogue must unfold within distinctive settings so readers can properly visualize everything as though they are there, taking part. We also know that these characters are traveling far outside of their territory due to local areas being claimed by others. All of this is told to us through dialogue, and not some long-winded exposition of events that are packaged in lines of narrative. This is how we create fluid momentum in stories and show constant action as the story develops. Long-winded narratives can bog down the telling of the story for the reader, effectively putting the brakes on the story movement. They'll want to take a break to grab a snack or turn on a TV. Instead, you want your action to be ceaseless, one scene after the next. And interesting, engaging dialogue helps to achieve this. It is important to know the motivations of your characters, however. You have to know what they want, and these motivations should come across in speech via action/reaction exchanges like the one that precedes these paragraphs.

Get to the Point

Dialogue in fiction, unlike that of real life conversation, should not be a discombobulated mess. It should be focused and direct, and come to some sort of point. In everyday conversations we tend to ramble and strike off in various directions before we come to an actual point (if ever we do). Dialogue, on the other hand, needs to come to a point, and without the needless baggage of stutters, pauses, and meanderings associated with real conversations. If you take a real conversation, clean it up, pare it down to its bare essentials, give it focus, and have it come to a point of some kind in the end, you'd have a decent scene for a novel. But a real conversation in and of itself won't do. Listening to how real people speak and interact with one another is important, however. Once you get a feel for how real people speak you can start to apply that to your own characters, giving them words with interesting phraseology that will help to form their individual personalities, as different characters must speak differently.

Dialogue in fiction has to feel authentic, as though real people are saying real things, but it can't be as haphazard as the real thing. Your goal is something close to the real thing, something believable, but with a cleaner, more focused delivery. And dialogue should never take place between two characters without anything of substance being said. Each time two or more of your characters converse, new information should be imparted and the plot advanced.

Bonus Point

Characters that say nothing of substance populate stories without substance. Dialogue should serve a purpose

Rises and Falls

Dialogue, much like your overall plot, should come with what I call "rises and falls," a term lifted from ballroom dancing. Just as one may lower his or her center of gravity with bends and sways, or raise it by pushing up on the balls of their feet, plot and dialogue should rise and fall where tension, drama, action, urgency, and other storytelling devices are concerned.

With plot and dialogue, things must escalate, become more tense or urgent as the story progresses. This is true whether we're dealing with a pregnancy we learn of at the outset of a story, which evolves to an actual birth by the story's end, or the threat of war that evolves into war itself. Tension, action, urgency, drama, you name it, will escalate as the story progresses. But you must also have rises and falls within individual scenes that deliver exchanges of dialogue. The dialogue must rise and fall like the tracing lines produced on the graph of an ECG machine. For an example of this we'll look at another scene from an episode of *Mafiosi* Season One. While celebrating the acquisition of a Brooklyn night spot at a mob-owed Manhattan club, our lead character Vincenzo is told to make nice with seasoned mobster Tony Gallo, who is upset about the way things were handled. We'll get the gist of the story from the dialogue exchange and study the rises and falls that occur throughout.

> Crowded tables surrounded the dance floor and stage, and in the far corner, all the way to the back of the club, is where we found Tony Gallo, sitting by himself. He was nursing a dark drink and surveying the room.
>
> He eyed us warily as we approached. When we stood over him, I asked if he'd mind if we sat down. ***(Always establish a clear setting where the dialogue is taking place.)***
>
> "Suit yourselves," he said in his damaged voice. "You two seem to do whatever you want these days." ***(Tension exists at the very start of the conversation, so our ECG tracing line ticks upward.)***
>
> We grabbed two chairs from nearby tables and sat with him.
>
> "Come on. What're you going on about?" I asked.
>
> "Yeah, what's this about you being sore at us?" Paul added. ***(The reaction of the two newcomers is mellow, in effect countering the bitter response from the veteran,***

wherein the tension exists. Our ECG line goes down a notch then straightens out.)

Tony Gallo set his drink on the table and looked at me. He looked at Paul, and then he turned back to me. "You two know what this is. You came to me about this thing, and I told you how it was gonna work, what it would take to have me sign on. Well, you done that. You done what I said to do, but then you turned your backs on the deal. I don't care that the terms are a bit different. So you're not breaking ground on something, you took over another establishment instead. So what? I don't sweat those kinds of details. What we talked about was me signing on once Carlo did. I said you get him to come in on this thing, I come in, simple as that. But what do you two do? Close the door in my face, that's what."

He sat back and scowled. ***(Our line traces back up again as the tension mounts.)***

I leaned back in my chair and considered his words. I glanced at Paul. He was as surprised as I was. I looked at Tony Gallo, who was still scowling.

"When we came to you, nothing was concrete," I said. "We were feeling around in the dark trying to get people to throw in. Truth is, you were the first person we came to out of respect. And you're right, you did carry us with the Milwaukee thing. That's why we came to you in the first place, but you didn't want to wet your beak. Those were your words." ***(This calm delivery sends our line back down a touch, but tension is still in the air. Note the information that is being imparted to advance the plot as well. This isn't just random dialogue. We're getting story tidbits.)***

Tony Gallo narrowed his eyes. "You don't have to

throw my words back at me. I remember what I said. But forget all that, 'cause you're twisting what I said anyways."

"Nobody's twisting anything," Paul said. ***(The line traces back up, but another character is increasing the tension.)***

"Here are the facts," Tony Gallo said. "You two just came into this thing of ours, so you're still wet behind the ears. I don't care how many lucky heists you roll out on, or how many civilian guineas you whack while they ain't looking. It's time put into this thing that earns you stones." He pointed a finger and waved it back and forth between us. "You ask me, you two got the luck o' the Irish, what with the bosses deciding to toss you into my ocean. Yeah, you're swimming with a shark, a made man. What other two wet-behind-the-ears *cugines* can claim that? You point 'em out." ***(Our line is stable at this point.)***

He had a point there. Paul and I shared a glance and kept listening. ***(Here, it goes down, and the tension decreases.)***

"You two have no idea what kind of advantages could fall into your lap swimmin' with me. You willing to turn your back on that? Here I am, coming to you two with something like this. I coulda just as easily had Carlo order you to give me a cut. But I ain't tryin' to muscle in on what you two are working for. I respect it, see? But you can't keep shoving me aside like I'm an *indegno*, no-brain dago, you hear?" ***(A small uptick. Just enough to keep the tension going.)***

I rubbed my chin and shared another glance with Paul. Then I fixed Tony Gallo with a serious look. "Here's the deal. You come in on this, you gotta bring something to the table, besides startup." ***(And down goes the tension line, but our curiosity is piqued.)***

His face softened for the first time since we'd approached his table. "Like what?" ***(The line traces down yet more.)***

"Like protection for the females," I said.

"Maybe bouncers," Paul threw in.

Tony Gallo screwed his face up. "I look like I run a security agency to you?" ***(One small uptick in our line.)***

"We're just tossing out ideas," I said.

"*All'inferno* with your ideas. This is what I'm saying here. You two are still new at this. You don't know how to delegate yet. You gotta learn people's strengths. For one thing, you come to me about starting up a club when I don't know the first thing about it, but that's beside the point. Carlo's brains are behind this thing now. What I'm sayin' is, you gotta zero in on an earner's strengths, then beef those up. So, this new spot, it got a basement?" ***(A small dip in our line occurs here.)***

"Yeah, it has a basement," Paul said. "Why?"

Tony Gallo picked up his drink and swirled it. The ice cubes rattled against the glass. "I'll set up a gambling operation down there. Blackjack tables, card games, I'll even throw in a few betting machines for the ladies and the old geezers. Top of the line."

Paul and I were grinning now. I nodded my approval. "Yeah, that's more like it." ***(The tension is completely gone, and the situation is diffused. Now our focus is on a new dynamic.)***

Tony Gallo took a few sips of his drink and then set it down. "That's what I do. People will eat it up. Plus it gives me another spot to seed."

"Now this is brilliance," I said.

Paul reached a hand across the table, and Tony Gallo shook it. "You're in," Paul said. "We definitely want you in."

I stuck out my hand, and Tony Gallo and I shook on the deal. It was official. He was on board with the Brooklyn strip club.

This scene is much like those scenes in films where an ordinary Joe is trying to diffuse a bomb based on instructions from supposed experts stationed offsite. Tension and suspense exist in the possibility of the wrong wire being cut and the bomb going off, but when the bomb is defused, we all breathe easy and enjoy the scene that plays out. The same holds true here. When there are rises and falls in your dialogue exchanges, coupled with information flows that reveal new things to the reader as well as elements that advance the plot, you've got the makings of a great scene of dialogue.

Worksheet 6

NOW LET'S SEE IF YOU'VE BEEN PAYING ATTENTION. IN THE SCENE BELOW, INDICATE WHERE AN ACTION AND A REACTION OCCURS, AS WELL AS RISES AND FALLS.

(Write either an A or R in the white boxes in the first column and an R or F in the boxes in the second.)

[Rexford] didn't bother to switch on the light, preferring to sit at his desk in the dark while giving his back to the spectacular views.

He initiated a call on his office phone and sat back in his chair as the line rang.

"Norman," said a male voice with a slight German accent. "Where are we?"

"We haven't located him yet, sir," Rexford said.

"Did you have Dahl point him to Geneva as we discussed?"

"Yes, but there's been no sign of him yet, which means he's probably not entering through normal channels. And, uh, Dahl was killed in Helsinki, by the way."

"*Unglaublich*! Have you put any good agents on him?" asked the man on the other end of the line.

"He dispatched them all, including Antoninus Gray, the best of the lot. We even lost the Russian girl in Pulkovo Airport, in a shower stall, of all places. And Ming Li—that is, Orchid—expired as well, among several other agents. Phase IIs seem to have no effect on him. That said, I think it was a mistake leading him to Geneva."

"This is unsettling news, Norman. Just who is this man?"

Rexford paused briefly as he considered the question. "That's just it, sir, he's still a man, capable though he is. We'll just have to find a way to put him down. He'll show up sooner or later."

The man on the other end of the line sighed. Finally he said, "We are not going to sit around and wait for him to show up on our doorstep. Send every agent we have and be done with it. There is no way he can manage that many at once."

"Are you sure you want that, sir?" Rexford asked, careful not to sound insubordinate. The very idea would mean risking the entire Red*rum* line and exposing their agenda to the world if the effort failed. Rexford didn't like it.

"You object?" the man asked.

"I just don't feel we're ready for that. Many of these agents are unseasoned, and a good percentage are still in the early stages of training and upgrades. And, as I said, our very best agents are dead. We risk exposure if anything were to go wrong. And it very well may, considering who we're dealing with, sir. I can't have that happen."

Worksheet 6

"And there it is," the man said. "*You* can't have that happen. But you're merely overseeing this operation. Whatever authority you have is granted by us."

"You're absolutely right, sir. I don't mean to overstep my bounds."

That seemed to soften the German's tone. "At any rate, I've heard your reasoning, and rest assured that I have considered it. The matter is settled. When we hang up, I want you to give the order. We'll dispatch a dozen Phase IIs instead. Does that work for you?"

"It does indeed, sir," Rexford said. "We've also found a way to jam his communication frequency, so he'll be unable to reach whoever has been helping him."

"Very good," the German said. "With that I will leave you. *Gute nacht, Herr* Rexford."

"Goodnight, Mr. Stauffenberg."

TAKEN FROM 711 PRESS TITLE *KILL FACTOR: SERPENT HEAD*

Point 7

Crafting Your Story

The Importance of Plot

The Importance of Plot

Character development is something I tend to look for most in novels, especially when the material is character-driven rather than plot-driven. If a story centers more on plot and action, then I will be inclined to lend greater consideration to the symmetry of the plot—whether there is a harmonious arrangement of the rudiments in the overall story; whether the story rises and falls with creative tension; and whether the author maintains a narrative and thematic balance. Be it character- or plot-driven, however, the story must be well-structured, being set inside a sturdy framework that includes a strong beginning, a captivating middle, and a satisfying end, with the usual character arcs and ebb and flow of events therein.

Martha Alderson, an author, teacher, and plot consultant, has this to say about writers who prefer to write either character-driven or plot-driven stories:

> *Broadly speaking, writers who prefer writing action-driven stories focus on logical thinking, rational analysis, and accuracy. Action-driven writers tend to rely more on the left side of their brain. These writers approach writing as a linear function and see the story in its parts. Action-driven writers like structure. They usually pre-plot or create an outline before writing. Action-driven writers have little trouble expressing themselves in words.*
>
> *On the other hand, writers who write character-driven stories tend to focus on aesthetics and feelings, creativity and*

imagination. These writers access the right side of their brains and enjoy playing with the beauty of language. They are more intuitive, and like to work things out on the page.

Interestingly enough, I am drawn to both models; but, as you would expect, for different reasons. Regardless of which side of the brain you the writer tend to tap into most, it is important that you have, at the very least, a loose view of the overall plot. If you don't know where your story is going, it may not be pleasant when you arrive at the final destination, particularly for the reader. Whether you arrive at that destination by mapping out your entire book with meticulous care, or you enjoy working things out on the page while relying on a loose plot, that's up to you. The point is that a plot is necessary.

Having said that, I will also say this: sticking faithfully to a plot is like thinking of driving a made-up route along imaginary roads in a country you've never visited or researched, only to actually arrive in that country and begin traveling their real roads while trying to stick to your imaginary route. You'll find that it is necessary to adapt to the road ahead of you and follow a trajectory you hadn't considered. Plotting a book is the same. Plots should not be set in stone; they should only act as guideposts along your story's winding path, because that plot will evolve and grow somewhat of its own accord as your tale unwinds and characters come to life. And there is no way you can clearly envision or foresee events that will occur down the stretch while you are mapping out the plot at the book's outset. Overplotting also bogs down a story.

> **BONUS POINT**
>
> Knowing the end from the beginning is important. A structured plot will enable you to do so

Of course, plotting has a great many detractors, those who view it as a crutch or a tool to be used only in utter desperation, but history has it that great plots have existed in the most popular tales in each and every era. Kate Mosse, an author who has taught a Guardian Masterclass on plot has this to say:

> *WHAT ARE THE OLDEST STORIES we know of? Aboriginal Dreamtime tales are rich in incident—the characters do things and their actions cause change. Greek myths are full of challenges faced and met by interchangeable heroes. In his Poetics, Aristotle himself refers to plot as the most important element of drama, trumping character or setting or even language. The 4th-century polymath coined the truism "beginning, middle and end" and recommended that the events should interconnect.*
>
> *Fast forward to 1863. Gustav Freytag developed Aristotle's three parts into five: exposition, rising action, turning point, falling action and resolution. The exposition introduces the main characters—who they are and what they want. The plot is about how they try to get it.*

Pound for pound, plots are important to storytelling. I'll go so far as to say that the plot itself is in fact the story. Without a plot, all you'd be left with are a series of events that involve the same characters. There wouldn't be a seamless journey with a beginning, middle, and end, but probably random, character-driven scenes that go nowhere and everywhere at once. You will have a story filled with characters that are floating aimlessly, and the story itself will have no end in sight, no solid destination, and no real anchor points to ground it. You don't want to have your characters floating aimlessly. You want them to have purpose, and you want the story to reach a satisfying conclusion. Consider the ending before you begin the story.

We human beings need goals. We need something to strive toward, something that fills us with a sense of purpose. Consider this: if you have ever held a job where you were given a menial task to accomplish, how much satisfaction did you gain from it? Even employers know that employees need something extra to keep them going. A good project manager will find meaningful tasks for their team members, and once those tasks are complete, he or she will find new tasks for them. We always look forward to new goals and are often given new tasks in life. We seek to earn diplomas and degrees, get a driver's license, land a challenging or interesting career. We become scientists with the hope of discovering something new, or doctors bent on finding the cure for diseases. In short, we need goals, tasks, and direction in life. Your characters do as well. So before you even jot down the first letter of the first word in your story or novel, you must consider where you're going with it before you get there. And most importantly, have an end in sight. This will be very conducive to forming a well-structured tale.

Plotting is planning, and it takes a good plan to accomplish most anything worthwhile. What's more, the plot is perhaps your first connection to the reader, the element that draws them in and keeps them hooked on your story.

One of the first things we read is the book blurb, which in most cases summarizes the main plot and gives us a taste of the overall story we can expect to encounter. At times a good plot summary is all it will take to pique our interest and get us to dive into a new tale. And when that tale gives us a little of what we expected, based on the plot or plan that was briefly laid out, we are satisfied that it met said expectations. Of course, the story elements that form the bigger picture, which cannot be condensed into a synopsis, will do the trick of taking things to the next level and exceed our expectations. But it is the plot that keeps us truly hooked. We want to see what will become of our hero or villain, whether a prize will truly be won or what consequences will arise from a poor decision or rash action. These are all clever plot devices, and they can be used to great effect to keep your readers turning the pages. That said, a writer must be careful to allow their plot to develop naturally and not force elements that will leave the story a contrived, overplotted mess. All of this takes a great deal of practice. You'll have to actually write, read, write, and read some more. In essence, you need to become a student of storytelling.

The Seven Basic Plots

According to British literary critic Christopher Booker, despite the untold number of tales that have ever been told, each can only fall within seven basic plots, which are as follows:

Overcoming the Monster: Your protagonist must confront a powerful, terrifying monster in a battle that may or may not end in death. Think *Beowulf*, *Jack and the Beanstalk*, and *Dracula*.

Rags to Riches: Your protagonist, a seemingly common individual by all accounts, is eventually shown to be in possession of a deeper more exceptional self. The riches here can be metaphoric as well as literal. Think *Cinderella*, *Jane Eyre*, *Superman*, *David Copperfield*, and *Pygmalion*.

The Quest: Upon learning of a priceless goal, your main character embarks on a perilous journey to reach it. Think *The Odyssey*, *The Count of Monte Cristo*, *Lord of the Rings*, *Moby Dick*, and *Raiders of the Lost Ark*.

Voyage and Return: Your main character or characters are whisked away to an unfamiliar setting or world that is different from the first, from which they are cut off. After an initial enchantment with this new world or setting, peril follows, leading to a dramatic escape and a return to the first familiar world. Think *Alice in*

Wonderland and *The Time Machine*, and more subtly in the simpler "leaving and returning home" sense of this plotline: *The Rime of the Ancient Mariner* and *Gone with the Wind.*

Comedy: Several of your characters are thrown together in a web of events that result in a knotted plot that has to be (and often is) unraveled by the end of the tale, which presents a happy ending. Think Shakespeare's comedies and almost anything by Jane Austen.

Tragedy: Your flawed main character is led on a fatal course than ends in disaster. Think the tragic ends of *King Lear, Madame Bovary, The Picture of Dorian Gray, Bonnie and Clyde,* and *Macbeth.*

Rebirth: A foreboding threat looms large over your main character, and he or she is held in the grip of darkness until they are redeemed or find a new reason for living through love or forgiveness or some other life-giving power. A myriad fairy tales anchor on this plot, as does *Crime and Punishment, A Christmas Carol,* and *It's a Wonderful Life.*

You can hang just about any story, novel, film, or play on one of these seven basic plots. And the book or story you will write can hang on one as well, if it is written thoughtfully. You should have a clear enough view of your story to know which basic plot it will hang on, however, so that you plan or plot it out with that in mind.

The first thing a story must do is hook the reader, if not from the very first sentence, then the first paragraph (and forbid that you don't do it there, let's aim for the first page at the very least). The idea is to center your entire story around an incident, from which the plot will develop. This should come early on. Some stories present it in the very first sentence—"It is a truth universally acknowledged, that a single man in possession of a good fortune must be in want of a wife." This is from *Pride & Prejudice,* whose story can be summed up in that one sentence. The story itself springs primarily out of an incident that is presented on the very first page. We hear of a man of great fortune named Bingley, who has taken residence nearby. What's more, he is said to be single, which is a fortunate business since there are several daughters of a marriageable age residing in the home of the central characters of this chapter.

So an initial story incident is of vital importance if you intend to hook your readers early on. The next thing you have to do is build on that initial incident, layering your plot with tension-filled scenes and character motivations that will propel them toward something for which you will create setbacks and complications. And all the while you will be thinking of where your story is going, what your characters will encounter, and how they will react to situations you will create. You will eventually see your story play out in your head like a film—beginning, middle, and end, and all you have to do is capture it on paper. Bring it to life. But that you will have to learn to do on your own. I can assure you that once you have a full view of your story, once it is fairly organized in your head or in plot form on paper, you will find that it is far easier to tell that story. It will flow from you like fond memories that have made indelible marks in your heart.

Set Design

In the film industry, set design is of paramount importance. Film actors, like stage actors, need a stage to work on, and the set designer is the one responsible for creating the most realistic and dynamic background for the actors so that their characters can come to life. If the stage is authentic enough, an actor can lose him- or herself in the make-believe world around them and deliver a memorable and moving performance. Set design is just as important in novels, but setting a literary scene is different from setting a literal one. When you place your character in a room or a desert or ski resort or wherever, that setting has to feel so authentic that the reader is actually transported into the character's body as they experience that particular scene.

As a writer, you will have to learn how to describe settings in a vivid way. Through the setting, you want to draw powerful feelings from your readers and plant strong, clear images in their minds. In the opening scenes of a Movie Book we released in 2011 called *Long, Cold Winter*, we get just such a scene, which paints a vivid picture of the New England forests the main characters drive through to get to a remote lodge.

> The winding back roads they had traveled since setting out at six o'clock that morning had provided a panorama of constantly changing and breathtakingly beautiful scenery. The forests were full of late autumn's lush colors, and clusters of red, orange, and yellow made for a dramatic vista. Between the collage of colors, evergreens filled the hills and valleys with splashes of emerald and jade and purified the air with their clean, piney scent.

New England is known for its stunning fall colors, and that is played up to great effect in the above scene description. Anyone who has driven similar roads in autumn will readily identify, and those who haven't will long to after reading the above.

If dialogue plays a part in the scene, you want to expand on the setting further by interspersing descriptions of it within the dialogue itself and through the eyes of your characters. This way, the setting is not just a pretty backdrop, but an integral part of the scene. Going back to *Kill Factor: Serpent Head*, we are presented with a nighttime scene in the beautiful French Riviera, where two characters, who have just met, are walking toward a popular marina as they feel each other out. The scene description that follows places us directly in the setting:

> The night air was crisp and sweet as it drifted in from the Mediterranean. As they talked, the two walked down to the marina and strolled along a crowded avenue before turning onto a narrow wharf that jutted out into the harbor. Several yachts were moored on either side of them, and they appeared unoccupied. When they came to the end of the wharf, the brisk, salty air of the French Riviera blew against Magenta's face as she admired the night sky. Above them, the moon's enchanting glow cast down its silver radiance, which shimmered atop the waters of the harbor.

There is no mistaking where these characters are or what the night air feels and smells like, but you don't have to spell that out in great detail, as it is already implied. As the scene continues, more dialogue is exchanged, and then the female character's attention is drawn elsewhere:

> Egli was looking at her profile, since her attention had been drawn to something out on the water. When he looked in the direction in which she was looking, he said, "In that case, what kind of conversation do you propose?" A yacht was anchored in the distance, a few lights shining along deck windows on its starboard side. They could hear what sounded like a faint commotion drifting toward them from the boat and music trailing through the air.
>
> "Do you think they are giving a party?" Magenta asked, changing the subject.

The scene description that is interspersed in the dialogue actually becomes a part of the conversation and is therefore an integral part of the scene. What's more, we are seeing it through the eyes of the characters. The next example is no different:

> "Perhaps. There are scores happening all around us as we speak," said Egli, sweeping his eyes over the buildings that rose out of the mountain landscape behind them. "We can go to one if you'd like.

As we can see from the above, dialogue can come to life if it is interspersed with actual setting information. For instance, in one of your conversations someone might place a cup down on a "Corian" countertop, or characters might be talking in an outdoor café setting when one of them notices a couple walking by and describes clothes that place us in the 1920s. Be mindful, however, that you do not want to intersperse random descriptions that are not integral to the plot or scene in question, or else do not go into great detail about people passing by. They can merely act as a time stamp or a moving backdrop that brings your setting to life. After all, the idea is to have the scene be as real and fleshed out as possible, which means sticking to details that bear that out and not straying from them.

With time and practice, you will begin to get a good sense of when and where to intersperse scene descriptions, how to create rises and falls in dialogue, and, in fact, how to apply all of the lessons contained in this book. But it will take just that: time and practice. Learning how to write, and write well, is not something that happens overnight. It will take a great deal of dedication and desire on your part, but it is possible. And the seven *Points* I have laid out here are just the start.

Here's to powerful storytelling!

Worksheet 7

In Your Own Words, Describe the Plot of the Most Memorable Story You Can Recall.
(Base your plot on something you read—a book or short story if possible.)

Which of the Seven Basic Plots Does the Story Above Fall Under?
(Select only one by placing a checkmark in one of the white boxes below.)

- [ ] Overcoming the Monster
- [ ] Rags to Riches
- [ ] The Quest
- [ ] Voyage and Return
- [ ] Comedy
- [ ] Tragedy
- [ ] Rebirth

Using the Lines Below, Plot a Future Flash Fiction Piece You Intend to Write.
(Make sure it is in the same basic plot category as the story above.)

Conclusion

You will note that the *7 Points of Write* are not a set of rules based on a paint-by-numbers writing system; rather, they are a set of principles, or literary philosophies, culled from years of editorial experience and publishing know-how. They are not a magic pill that will grant you writing expertise overnight. Everything that is presented in this book is essentially a primer, a jumping off point in your extended quest to achieve storytelling greatness. It is up to you, the writer, to apply these principles in your everyday writing and study your craft.

While this book is aimed at fiction writers, particularly those interested in writing novels, we run a publishing company with a unique set of rules. For one, novels tend to run between 75,000 and 100,000 words, so we don't refer to our books as "novels" or approach fiction writing from an industry standpoint, where a plot has to take up a week's worth of material (if one were to read at a normal pace). Through 711 Press, we instead publish what we call Movie Books, which contain stories that are meant to be consumed in the same amount of time it takes you to watch an actual film or television show. And while the mediums differ, our Movie and TV Books apply the same storytelling conventions used in film and television productions. Certain themes are explored, plot arcs are carried over, and characters are given room to develop and grow as the narrative unspools during the course of your reading. But all this doesn't take a week to experience, since our books, as I said, take the same amount of time to read as watching a movie or television show does.

So what is said herein is really for those who want to tell organic stories that form out of natural events you recount in a seamless narrative. We don't believe in paint-by-numbers writing formulas or exaggerated word and page counts that force writers to artificially inflate their stories for the sake of minimum requirements, which only creates novel "filler." If you have a story to tell, tell it. But let it happen naturally, or as naturally as possible. You can learn how to do that with practice and study.

Also, be aware that the experience gained from actually writing a novel or a series of stories cannot be replaced or replicated. You have to be in the moment, knee-deep in the creative process to allow these seven *Points* to take root. A writer writes, period. No matter how many workshops you attend or how many books you read on writing, it will take actual practice to learn your craft and become good at it. In fact, in order to become good at anything—scuba diving, driving a car, riding a bike, speaking a new language—it doesn't matter how many lessons you take. What really teaches you is experience.

As I've said, great writers aren't born, they're made, and just about anyone can learn how to tell a compelling story if they have drive and direction. Most importantly, however, you have to be a student of storytelling, and that means imbibing it in all of its various forms. Go to plays, watch movies and TV shows, listen to audio books, and read, read, read. Read as often as you can, and as diverse a collection of material as you can. Read newspapers, how-to books, novels, short stories, and pay attention to how the words flow on the pages, where punctuations fall, and note the points that are being brought forth. Pay attention to themes and narrative flows and how the story is unfolding or building, and concentrate on dialogue exchanges and word usage. Read at least seven times the amount of writing you achieve in one day (seven paragraphs for one paragraph of written material, seven pages for one page you write, etc.).

Note also that the world itself is your school, so study the people and things around you. You can glean valuable information by doing so. This is what great painters have done. Life is actually speaking to you; life is always teaching you, but you have to be open and attuned to the things that it's showing you. Your eyes have to be open, and your ears have to be open. Say you want to write a hospital scene; instead of researching where tubes go, what machines are in the room, or what the medical terminology is for this and that, first tap into a past experience that involves a hospital setting and relive that experience through your scene. Think about what it felt like when a close friend or relative was sick. Remember what you felt inside, and let the emotions flow through your fingers. In short, learn from life, listen to life as it speaks to you, and tap into the things you've seen and experienced firsthand. In time, you'll begin to write with ease, and words will form wonderful sentences right before your eyes, and those sentences will combine to form paragraphs that will convey meaningful thoughts and interesting ideas to your readers.

Before you know it, you'll have a book on your hands, and one that contains a very compelling story that is all your own.

About the Author

Daniel Middleton began his career in book publishing in 2001, by proofreading and copyediting galley proofs for a small Brooklyn-based press. Since that time, Mr. Middleton, in addition to editing a variety of works, has developed a love of graphic design and has become an accomplished book designer in his own right, heading up a book design company he launched in 2005 called *Scribe Freelance*. Through his company, he has had the good fortune of working with a number of successful self-published authors and small presses with unique offerings.

Recently, he decided to parlay his collective publishing experience into a new publishing company, *711 Press,* which has released this publication and will focus solely on new works of fiction.

Daniel Middleton resides in New York with his loving wife and adoring daughter.

CPSIA information can be obtained at www.ICGtesting.com
Printed in the USA
LVOW10s1007071214

417623LV00001B/179/P

9 781935 702108